Victorian Britain

VICTORIAN CRIME

Fiona Macdonald

FRANKLIN WATTS
LONDON•SYDNEY

First published in 2009
by Franklin Watts

Copyright © 2009 Franklin Watts

Franklin Watts
338 Euston Road
London NW1 3BH

Franklin Watts Australia
Level 17/207 Kent Street
Sydney, NSW 2000

Dewey classification number 364.941

ISBN 978 0 7496 8679 6

Planning and production by Discovery Books Limited
Editor: Helen Dwyer
Design: Simon Borrough

Printed in China

Franklin Watts is a division of Hachette Children's Books,
an Hachette UK company. www.hachette.co.uk

Photo credits:
Discovery Picture Library: pp. 6, 8, 9 top, 10, 17, 18; Getty Images:
p. 5 (Hulton Archive); Inveraray Jail: pp. 14 top, 19 left, 28; Mary
Evans Picture Library: 7, 9 bottom, 11, 12, 13, 16, 20, 22, 23, 24,
25, 26, 27, NCCL Galleries of Justice. p. 21, Shutterstock: p. 15
(Stephen Finn); Staffordshire Past Track: pp. 4 (Staffordshire Arts
and Museum Service), 19 right (Staffordshire Arts and Museum
Service); Tim Locke: p.29; www.picturethepast.org.uk: 14 bottom
(Nottingham City Council)

CONTENTS

CRIME ON THE
❋
INCREASE

The Victorian age began in 1837 when Princess Victoria became Queen and ended when she died in 1901. At the start of Queen Victoria's reign, Britain was a fast-growing, fast-changing nation. It had new industries based on steampower, new towns and cities, new roads and railways and new mines and factories. Overseas, it was taking control of a mighty empire. Britain was both rich and strong – but it was also facing a crime crisis.

Crime increased, year by year, until around 1850. By then, there were over 20,000 reported crimes each year. Many others were never reported. Theft (stealing) was the most common offence, and murder was the most rare (around 400 cases a year). Violence was common, even against women and children. Many men carried knives for protection, or sharp tools used for their work.

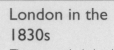

London in the 1830s

The scoundrels had everywhere the upper hand – in the streets, in the suburbs, and on the river. The roads leading to and from the metropolis [capital city] were infested by thieves and footpads [thieves on foot]. It was unsafe to walk abroad anywhere after nightfall. The thieves were much better organised than the police. There were day thieves and night thieves … duck-hunting and dog-fighting went on in public thoroughfares [streets] by day, and after dark the streets were disgraced by broils [brawls] and disturbances, making night hideous.

The Quarterly Review, 1868.

Gnosall, Staffs. The old Lock Up.

The grey stone building on the left of this picture is the lock-up (small local prison) in the village of Gnosall, Staffordshire. In was built in 1830 to hold minor criminals, such as beggars, tramps and drunks.

In this 1851 illustration, a highwayman armed with a pistol takes two travellers by surprise on a country lane and frightens them into giving him their money.

City crime

In cities, there were burglars, **muggers**, shop-lifters, pickpockets and all kinds of fraudsters and tricksters. The many poor people, including children who lived on the streets, were also treated as criminals.

Country crime

In the countryside, there was **poaching**, sheep-stealing and, sometimes, highway robbery. Mobs of farm workers protested against unemployment and low wages by smashing new farm machines or setting fire to valuable produce.

Fighting crime

There was no national, organised police force to detect or fight against these crimes. Instead, cities and villages relied on local constables (poorly paid law-officers) and **night watchmen** to catch criminals and put them on trial.

Where You Live

The names of prisons and other places of punishment that disappeared long ago are preserved in many place names. Go to your local library and find a street map or road atlas of your town or city, or else a large scale map of the area around your school. Study them carefully, using an index if there is one. Can you find any names linked with crime, such as 'Hangman's Hill', '**Gaol Street**' or '**Gallows Corner**'?

United Kingdom, Separate Laws

The text in this book describes crime and the law in England and Wales. In Queen Victoria's time, Scotland and Ireland had their own separate laws and law courts. Today, many laws in Scotland and Northern Ireland are still different from the rest of the UK.

POVERTY AND CRIME

New industries and new ways of working created wealth for successful Victorians. But most work in factories, mines, brickworks, potteries and other industries was poorly paid. The gap between rich and poor people widened in Victorian times.

This early 19th-century cartoon shows Britannia (a woman symbolising the British nation) asleep and doing nothing to help, while poor people (shown at the back of the picture) are suffering.

Poor relief

In the early 19th century, unlike today, the government did not provide money to help people who could not find work, or who were too young, old, or ill to support themselves. Instead, each parish (local community) gave money – called poor relief – to pay for feeding and housing its poor people.

But poverty was increasing throughout the countryside: prices rose, wages fell and farmworkers were unemployed and starving. Many parishes protested that paying poor relief was too expensive. They also claimed that money payments made poor people lazy.

Workhouses

In 1834, Parliament passed a New Poor Law, which stayed in force for all Queen Victoria's reign. It said that poor people should be locked up in **workhouses** (huge buildings like prisons), as if they were criminals. They could be given food to keep them alive, but only if they worked for it. Workhouse inmates had to obey strict rules: men and women – even married couples – had to live separately. If a poor person died in a workhouse, their body could be cut up for medical research – even if this was against their religious beliefs. For many poor Victorians, having to enter a workhouse was at least as bad as going to prison, so a life of crime was often considered a better option.

Parliament hoped that these grim workhouse conditions would stop people asking for poor relief. Instead, many poor, helpless people lived in terror of being sent to the workhouse. To find work – and to avoid the workhouse – millions of country people moved to industrial cities early in Victoria's reign.

Cut off from the Community

By 1850, for the first time ever, more than half the British population lived in cities or towns. Newcomers to big cities were no longer surrounded by their families, friends and neighbours. No-one knew them or cared what they did. Without their community to guide and warn them – and because workhouse conditions were so terrible – it was dangerously easy for some to get caught up in crime.

Mealtime in the men's section of the Marylebone workhouse in London in 1900. Even at the end of Victorian times, conditions in workhouses were little better than in prisons.

IN THE UNDERWORLD

Victorian cities grew quickly, with little planning. Streets for rich people were wide and tree-lined, but poor working people lived in rows of badly-built terraced houses. There were also foul city **slums**, with no water, drains or sewers.

In this 'underworld', stinking rubbish was piled high in the streets; rats and cockroaches scurried through half-ruined houses, shabby courtyards and dark, twisting alleys.

The world of the slums

The poorest of the poor lived here: abandoned women, children and old people, sick or injured workers, people with mental problems and people who had lost all their money and possessions. Slums were also safe hiding places for anyone on the run: escaped prisoners, army deserters and servants hiding from cruel masters. Surrounded by filth and misery, they could lie low for weeks. Few law-abiding citizens dared to enter the slum underworld to look for them because it was too dangerous.

Poor men, women and children crowd into a shabby room in London. They are watching two thieves play – and probably cheat at – a late-night game of cards.

Crime for a living

There were also tough professional criminals in all Victorian cities. They trained teams of pickpockets, sold stolen goods, blackmailed innocent people and ran **protection rackets**, demanding money from working families and traders. If victims did not pay up, their homes or shops were destroyed. Many professional criminals could be hired to kill or kidnap; others arranged for crimes to be committed. There were also many wild, lawless children, who had never known any other way of life.

Trapped in crime

If newcomers to big cities could not find work or pay for decent lodgings, they might easily end up in slums – and become criminals, just to stay alive. They might steal food, or work for a gang, or try begging, which was illegal. Once they entered the criminal underworld, it was almost impossible to escape. They were trapped in a life of crime.

Underworld Stories

Charles Dickens (1812–1870) was the most popular writer in early Victorian England. Dickens' father spent years in prison for **debt**, so Dickens had to work as a boy in a grim London factory to survive. He used many of his own experiences to make his stories true-to-life. Many of his best-loved stories describe the criminal underworld. In *Oliver Twist* the character Fagin runs a gang of child pickpockets, while Bill Sykes is a violent criminal and a murderer. In *Great Expectations*, Magwitch is a criminal who has escaped from a prison ship.

A Group of Child Prisoners

There were fourteen of them in all, some with shoes, some without … for trial on the charges of pocket-picking, and fourteen such villainous faces we never beheld. There was not one redeeming feature among them – not a glance of honesty – not a wink of anything expressive of anything but the gallows and the hulks [prison ships] in the whole collection. As to anything like shame or contrition [remorse], that was entirely out of the question.

Charles Dickens, *Sketches by Boz*, 1836.

Illustrations for Charles Dickens' Oliver Twist *show gangland thief and murderer Bill Sykes trying to escape over the rooftops (top) and the Artful Dodger teaching Oliver to pick the pockets of the rich (above).*

POLITICS AND PROTEST

The 19th century was a time of political unrest in many parts of Europe. Many people wanted political and social reform. Protesters were often treated as criminals and punished severely.

The Chartists

The **Chartists** (active from 1836 to 1858) wanted changes to government, such as votes for all men over 21 and secret voting. Their leaders organised **petitions**, held mass-meetings and published newspapers calling for political reform.

Most Chartists opposed violence, but they were still put in prison. A few Chartists called for direct action and organised riots. The government used armed troops to crush them. In Newport, south Wales, for example, 14 protesters were killed in 1839, and the local Chartist leader was **transported** to Australia.

Trade unions

In 1799, laws were passed that made it illegal for someone to belong to a trade union. Members of trade unions (organised groups of workers) called for ordinary peoples' rights. They demanded better pay,

*The Newport Riots, 1839. Chartists (right), using home-made guns and weapons, fight with soldiers and volunteers guarding the Westgate Hotel in Newport, south Wales. A suspected **Chartist** organiser had been imprisoned there, by the town's mayor.*

shorter working hours and safer working conditions. They held meetings and **strikes**. For example, in 1842, miners in Staffordshire, mill workers in Lancashire and many other workers around the country went on strike to protest about their working conditions and pay.

Most union members were law-abiding, but a few clashed violently with non-union workers, employers and the police. For example, in Sheffield in 1866, union members were accused of arson (setting fire to buildings) and murder.

Support for Strikes

From 1871, trade unions were fully recognised by law and their members had the right to strike for better pay and working conditions. In 1888, women matchmakers went on strike to improve their working conditions and pay. In the following year, London's poorly paid dock workers also went on strike for more money. They took part in large, peaceful processions. Both groups of workers won the sympathy of the public. The strikes also made many middle-class people aware that unskilled workers were badly paid.

The Rebecca Riots

In Wales, gangs of angry farmers and working men broke the law to protest about the high cost of tolls (charges for using roads) that were collected by private companies. Tolls made it extremely expensive to take goods to or from market, and threatened the survival of many poor, hard-working families.

From 1839 to 1844, men disguised as women made night raids to attack gates across toll-roads, threatening the gate-keepers and smashing the gates to pieces. They called themselves 'Rebecca and her Daughters', after a story from the Bible. Their protests led Parliament to set up an enquiry into unfair road tolls, and, in 1844, most tolls were **abolished**.

In May 1871, London matchmakers took part in a procession to protest at their working conditions. Afterwards the protesters complained that the police had been violent towards them.

11

THE POLICE

At the start of Queen Victoria's reign, there were no official police forces. The many different city and county councils each tried to combat crime and catch criminals in its own way.

Government leaders, members of parliament and voters were all worried by rising levels of crime. They demanded that 'something must be done' to improve law and order and safeguard honest citizens.

The first police force

In 1829, Sir Robert Peel, the **home secretary**, set up a new Metropolitan (capital city) police force in London. It employed police constables – soon nicknamed 'Bobbies' or 'Peelers' – in a planned, well-organised way. Peel's policemen wore uniforms (helmets and long blue coats) so that the public could recognise them. They carried **truncheons** and made regular street patrols (12 kilometres in daytime, 3 kilometres at night). They tried to prevent crime as well as chasing offenders. Within a year, there were almost 3,000 police constables watching over the streets of London. The Metropolitan Police had senior and junior ranks – and strict discipline – rather like the army.

Three young men get into a fight with two night watchmen in London in 1817. Twelve years later, London watchmen were replaced with an organised police force.

A slow start

At first, the public were suspicious. They thought that the new policemen were government spies, looking for poor people to send to workhouses. And the first police recruits were not all honest, or capable. One was sacked after only four hours at work – for drunkenness. But slowly, the new Metropolitan Police won respect, and became a model for other parts of Britain to copy.

Police throughout the country

In 1835, 1839 and 1840, new laws were passed allowing local councils to set up their own forces, similar to the Metropolitan Police. By 1855, around 12,000 new constables had been recruited. In 1856, the Police Act made sure that there were policemen in all regions and set up systems for checking and inspecting them.

Police Work

In *Dickens' Dictionary of London*, by Charles Dickens, Jr., 1879, the author lists 'public nuisances' that the police had to deal with. They included the following:

- Baiting animals
- Bonfires in streets
- Careless driving of cattle
- Cock-fighting
- Defacing buildings
- Exercising horses to annoyance of persons
- Discharging firearms
- Throwing fireworks in streets
- Playing games in streets
- Extinguishing lamps
- Mat-shaking after 8 am
- Musicians in streets
- Projections from houses to cause annoyance
- Ringing door bells without excuse
- Stone-throwing

A very early photograph, probably taken around 1850, of a group of policemen. Nineteenth-century police uniforms were not the same as today's. How many differences can you see?

COURTS AND TRIALS

People accused of minor crimes such as theft were tried by **magistrates,** who listened to the evidence then decided whether the accused should be punished or set free.

Quarter sessions

More serious cases were heard at courts called quarter sessions (because they were held four times a year) by magistrates plus a **jury** of 12 ordinary men who listened to the evidence and then gave their opinion. Women were only allowed to be jurors (jury members) from 1920.

This is a mace, which would be carried into the court in front of the judge as a symbol of his authority.

Assize courts

Serious crimes like **fraud** and murder were tried by trained royal judges, who travelled round the country, holding **assize courts** in all major cities and towns, two or three times each year.

Jurors listened to evidence from accused people and **witnesses** and to speeches by specially trained lawyers. Then the judge reminded the jurors of all the most important evidence in the case – and sometimes let them know his own opinions. After this, the jury had to decide if the accused person was innocent or guilty.

Judges arrive in Nottingham to try prisoners accused of serious crimes in 1895. They are riding in a grand golden coach, pulled by horses, to impress onlookers with the power and majesty of the law.

Where You Live
Victorian buildings still survive in the centre of many cities and towns. They include police stations and law courts. Many courts are decorated with statues of Justice (a blindfolded woman holding a pair of scales, evenly balanced). The most famous Victorian police station is the old Scotland Yard in London, which was closed in 1967.

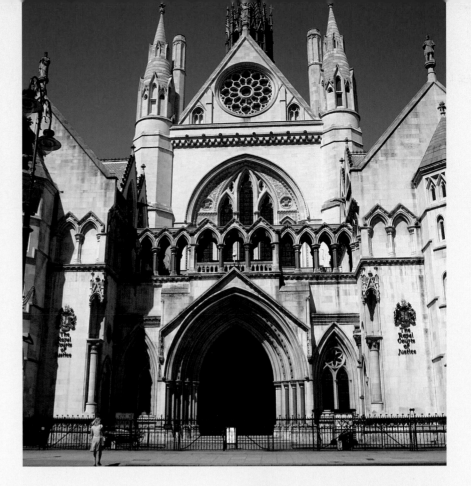

The Royal Courts of Justice in London were opened by Queen Victoria in 1882. Today, this is where some of the most serious criminal cases are heard.

If a criminal felt that their **conviction** was unjust, they had no way of making an appeal. All they could hope to do was beg the queen for a royal pardon. Victoria handed the duty to decide on these appeals to the home secretary.

Prosecutions

If you were a victim of crime in early Victorian times, it would be your responsibility to **prosecute** the criminal who had harmed you. There were no government prosecutors to speak up for victims or to bring accused criminals to court, except in Scotland. Rich people paid lawyers to prosecute suspected criminals for them.

In 1879, the British government created a new, senior, law officer: the director of public prosecutions. Lawyers working for him brought accused criminals to court – but only in serious cases.

No Justice for the Poor?
Poor people could not afford to pay lawyers. As a result, crimes against the poor often never got to trial and went unpunished. Many people complained that justice was only for the rich, and that judges, magistrates and lawyers were sometimes unfair, careless or lazy. One early Victorian newspaper voiced many people's feelings when it claimed: 'There is scarcely a court in the width and breadth of the land that is not a disgrace to the country!'

PUNISHMENTS

At the start of Victoria's reign, the chance of a crime being detected was low, and many criminals escaped unpunished. But for those who were caught and found guilty, punishments were usually severe.

Victorian people believed that criminals should suffer for doing wrong – and that their sufferings should be a warning to others. Convicted criminals might be flogged (beaten), sentenced to hard labour (such as building roads) or forced to join the navy.

Transportation

Many convicts were transported – sent far away from home to British-ruled lands overseas, especially Australia. Under armed guard, convicts crowded onto battered sailing ships for the long ocean voyage. Conditions on board were miserable, and many men and women died. If convicts survived to reach Australia, they were sent in gangs to clear land for farming, build docks and houses or work as servants. When they had served their sentences, they were usually free to stay in Australia or return home.

In this illustration from 1872, a criminal is flogged with lashes from the 'cat of nine tails' – a whip with nine strands of rope.

By the 1830s, one-third of all convicted criminals were transported overseas. But transportation was growing unpopular. It cost the government a lot of money and harmed innocent families left behind in Britain. Australia did not want any more convicts. The last transport ship sailed in 1867.

Hanging

Until 1823, over 200 crimes were punishable by hanging – a cruel and horrible way to die. Some 'hanging crimes' were serious, like murder; others were minor, such as house-breaking or sheep-stealing. Judges, politicians and the public felt that this was wrong, so in 1823 and 1830, the number of hanging crimes was reduced to under 100. In 1860, the law was changed again. Hanging remained the punishment for only four crimes: treason (trying to overthrow the government), murder, piracy and destroying national arsenals (weapons stores) or dockyards. Between 1800 and 1900, 3,542 people were hanged in England and Wales. The death penalty for crime was finally abolished in Britain in 1965.

This 19th-century cartoon shows an Australian outback farmer (right) complaining to a British policeman. He says: 'Don't shoot [send] any more of your rubbish [convicts] here, or you and I shall quarrel.'

GRIM PRISONS

As hanging and transportation became less popular, Victorian governments had to find other ways of punishing the growing number of criminals. They decided to lock them away in prisons.

Debtors' prisons and local gaols

Before Victorian times, prison was an unusual punishment in Britain. Normally, only **debtors** were locked up for long periods, along with suspects awaiting trial. Most towns and cities only had a small, local gaol – often known as a 'house of correction'.

Building new prisons

New, bigger, better prisons were obviously needed. In 1844, the government built a huge new national gaol, Pentonville, in London – and by 1850 there were 53 more. These new prisons were designed to humiliate prisoners and take away their dignity. At Pentonville, for example, inmates had to wear masks and were given numbers, not names. But they did have free time for reading, exercise and prayers.

Prison punishments

In 1865, a new Prisons Act set down even tougher rules for treating convicts in national and local gaols. Prisoners could

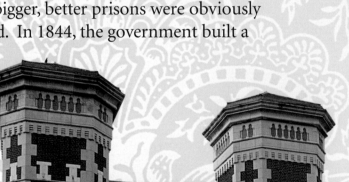

Prison Hulks

Until new prisons were built, the government sent convicts to 'hulks' – old, rotting, navy ships moored in the River Thames, in London. Convicts were chained to the ships' bunks day and night, or ferried to dry land and forced to do hard labour. The hulks were infested with disease-carrying rats and lice, so being sent there could be a death sentence. The last hulk was destroyed by fire in 1857.

The towering gateway of Wormwood Scrubs prison, London, built in 1875, was meant to frighten prisoners, as well as keep them inside the gaol.

Actors in 19th century clothes portray a prison warder locking a convict inside the cramped, miserable 'airing yard' at Inveraray Jail, Scotland. By law, prisoners were allowed fresh air and exercise – but they were not meant to enjoy it!

Prisoners at the treadmill (also known as a treadwheel) around 1870. Each man had to keep stepping as the wheel turned round. It was exhausting and very, very boring. The man seated at the left has been allowed to take a short break. Then he must go on stepping – for hours.

be chained to walls or handcuffed. Otherwise, they were forced to work for hours at exhausting, often pointless tasks, such as breaking stones, walking on a treadmill, or turning a heavy crank-handle. Disobedient prisoners could be locked in punishment cells, beaten, fed on bread and water only, or locked up for weeks in solitary confinement (alone). But a few rules aimed to help prisoners: each man or woman was meant to have their own separate cell; and each prison had its own doctor and priest.

In 1877, a second Prisons Act said that all prisons in Britain must come under government control. For the first time, government ministers could make rules about how all British prisons should be run, and all prisoners should be treated.

Where You Live

Some Victorian workhouses and prison buildings still survive today. Some workhouses became hospitals or have been converted into luxury flats, warehouses, or arts centres, but many Victorian prisons are still used to house criminals. The best way to find Victorian buildings in your area is to ask at your local studies library or go online.

CALLS FOR REFORM

Not all Victorians agreed that life in prison should be brutal and degrading. They suggested that time in prison should not be wasted on pointless tasks, but used to encourage prisoners to lead good lives.

Elizabeth Fry

The first prison **reformers** began work before Victoria became queen. The most famous was Elizabeth Fry (1780–1845). From 1813 to 1845, Fry campaigned to provide separate prisons for men and women, for female warders (to stop male warders harassing prisoners) and for schools for children who were locked up with criminal mothers. She set up classes to teach women prisoners how to read and sew; she hoped these skills

Reform campaigner Elizabeth Fry reads passages from the Bible to female prisoners in Newgate Prison, London.

A Reformed Prison

… at Broadmore there was a great barrack room, and with beds ranged round, and there we slept and messed, free to talk and amuse ourselves in a quiet way … The food was plentiful and excellent, contrasting strangely with that allowed the poor folks at the workhouses … They allow your hair and whiskers to grow at Broadmore … The work there is field and garden work … You get half a day's schooling a week, chapel twice a day … and two hours' exercise on Sunday. I was at Broadmore three months … I liked it very much indeed.

An interview with a prisoner in James Greenwood (1832–1929), *The Wilds of London*, 1874.

would help women find jobs after prison. Fry held Bible readings for prisoners and recruited teams of Christian volunteers to visit prisoners and help them.

Social and economic issues

Later reformers were inspired by political ideas. For example, Sir Edwin Chadwick (1800–1890) thought that helping prisoners to lead law-abiding lives would be good for the whole of society. **Economists** said that it was costly and pointless to imprison people for debt. They believed it was better to let criminals work hard and repay what they owed.

Helping children

In 1838, the first prison for young people was opened, but inmates were treated as harshly as adult prisoners. Children's welfare workers argued that young offenders needed help to learn how to be honest adults. In 1854, reform schools were set up to encourage and train young criminals to get jobs. From 1866, new industrial schools provided training in useful work skills for children thought to be at risk of becoming criminals.

[Some criminals] *are utterly weary of the hazard, disgrace and suffering attaching to their mode of life … they are frequently filled with bitter remorse, and make the strongest vows to have done with a guilty life … Suppose a man of this sort is in prison. He comes out of prison determined to reform. But where is he to go? What is he to do? How is he to live? Whatever may have been done for him in prison is of little or no avail, if as soon as he leaves the gaol he must go into the world branded with crime, unprotected and unhelped.*

James Greenwood (1832–1929), *The Seven Curses of London*, 1869.

(Far left) Here is Maud Pell, a young girl whose parents were both criminals, photographed before she was sent to reform school. She holds her hand out to beg for money, carries a bottle of beer and is dressed in dirty rags. She looks frightened and is frowning.

(Left) Here is Maud again, after years at reform school. She is clean and smartly dressed. She no longer needs to beg – the school has taught her skills to help earn her living. Maud no longer frowns, but she still looks rather nervous. If only we knew what she was thinking!

21

NEW KINDS OF CRIMES

Changes in industry and society in Victorian Britain led to several new kinds of crime. Criminals quickly found many new opportunities for doing wrong.

Industrial and commercial crime

New industries, and the growth of cities, meant that there were now many new goods all close together and ready to steal, in factories, docks and warehouses. New city banks had vaults (underground stores) full of money. Each week, on payday, millions of workers walked home with wages in their pockets.

New businesses created new opportunities for 'clever' commercial crimes, such as **embezzlement** and **fraud**. Dishonest lawyers or clerks stole clients' money; shopkeepers cheated customers by selling fake goods or polluted foods – such as bread made with powdered chalk (it was cheaper than wholesome flour).

Customers in a busy town bank in 1899. The new banks stored large amounts of money, and customers were putting in and taking out money all day long. This made banks an ideal target for thieves.

Crime Writing

In Victorian times, cheap magazines greatly increased public awareness of crime. Many, such as the popular 'penny dreadful' magazines, were full of shocking text and pictures about the most violent crimes. Even serious newspapers carried sensational reports of the latest police arrests and criminal trials. More seriously, new government statistics provided accurate, nationwide information about different kinds of crime and the number of criminals caught and sent to prison.

A London police sergeant and his constable investigate a break-in at a wealthy person's home. They believe it is the work of a gang.

Burglers and pickpockets

Successful business people were also new victims of crime. Rich families built splendid new houses in exclusive city streets and filled them with paintings, fine furnishings, silverware and jewellery. These became tempting targets for expert, professional burglars and thieves. City shops were stocked with valuable goods that attracted shop-lifters. Pickpockets mingled with crowds at fashionable theatres and racecourses, and in cheap, popular music-halls and public houses. Poor people's badly built homes were easy for burglars to break into.

Prosecuting employers

Victorian laws that aimed to protect workers and improve public life also created new kinds of crime. For the first time, owners of factories, mines and other work-places could be prosecuted for breaking rules on health and safety or working hours, and for polluting the environment.

THE FIRST DETECTIVES

By the second half of the 19th century, Britain's new police force had become larger, better organised and respected. As well as patrolling the streets, policemen were also being called to investigate and track down culprits.

Plain clothes detectives

Examining crime scenes for clues and tracing criminals were time-consuming and needed special skills. So, in 1842, the Metropolitan Police in London employed the first trained detectives in Britain. They wore plain clothes to work in secret and often put on disguises. Unlike earlier private investigators, who often had close links with criminals, most police detectives were honest and reliable. They became very popular. In 1856, a new law encouraged all police forces to follow the Metropolitan example and start detecting crimes.

Detective Fiction

Detective stories were invented in Victorian times. Readers loved pitting their wits against each new book's criminals. One of the first fictional detectives was Police Inspector Bucket, mentioned in Charles Dickens' novel *Bleak House* in 1855. The first proper detective story was *The Moonstone*, written by Wilkie Collins (1824–1889) in 1868. Its detective hero, Sergeant Cuff, was based on a real policeman. Sherlock Holmes, the world's most famous detective, was a private investigator. He was created by writer Arthur Conan Doyle (1859–1930) for his story *A Study in Scarlet*, published in 1887.

The blood-red cover of an early Sherlock Holmes detective story, The Sign of Four, *published in 1890.*

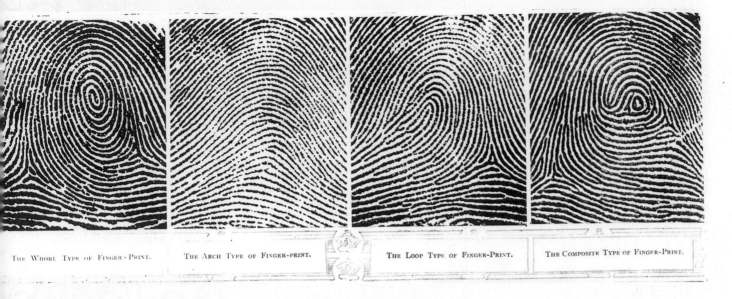

THE WHORL TYPE OF FINGER-PRINT.   THE ARCH TYPE OF FINGER-PRINT.   THE LOOP TYPE OF FINGER-PRINT.   THE COMPOSITE TYPE OF FINGER-PRINT.

Some of the earliest fingerprints taken by the Metropolitan Police. Anyone can be identified by their fingerprints because no two are alike.

The Task of Sherlock Holmes

There's the scarlet thread of murder running through the colourless skein [coiled thread] of life, and our duty is to unravel it, and isolate it, and expose every inch of it.

The detective Sherlock Holmes in *A Study in Scarlet*, 1887, by Arthur Conan Doyle

Nationwide records

In 1869, a National Criminal Record was set up. For the first time, there was a nationwide database of criminals and crimes. This helped local police forces share information and compare findings. It also let police superintendants (managers) plan regular patrols and special operations, and detectives could discover patterns of crime or track the activities of known offenders. In 1877, London detectives were organised into a new Criminal Investigation Department (CID) with 200 officers, and 600 further detectives were added in 1883.

Photographs and fingerprints

Towards the end of Victoria's reign, new technology helped detectives trace and arrest criminals. From the 1870s, criminals' faces were recorded, using new, cheap, black-and-white photography. Photographs helped police identify suspects, pass information all round the country and issue warning or 'wanted' posters. In 1901, police began to search for fingerprints at the scene of each serious crime after it was discovered that each person's prints are unique and can be used to identify them.

UNDERSTANDING CRIME

The Victorians liked facts. They were keen to study and understand. Victorian thinkers, scientists and politicians all began to ask: 'What causes crime?'

Inheritance and appearance

Many Victorians thought that some people were 'born to be bad'. They supposed (wrongly) that criminal behaviour could be passed on genetically from parents to children. Even more shocking, they believed that men and women who became criminals belonged to a 'lower' type of humanity than law-abiding people. They even tried to identify criminals from their physical appearance, suggesting, for example, that low eyebrows made a person 'brutish' (like an animal).

Phrenology

Phrenology is a fake science. It was invented in the 18th century and became fashionable in Victorian Britain. Phrenologists believed that bumps and lumps in the skull bones revealed how the brain inside had developed. They also thought that different areas of the brain controlled different types of behaviour – and that criminals would have extra-large bumps over brain-areas devoted to crime.

I feel as if I wanted something new to amuse me, and Mamma says it's because I've got such an active brain.

A drawing from 1890 makes fun of a lecture on phrenology.

Criminals or victims?

Today, science has proved that those opinions are wrong. Even in Victorian times, some people did not believe them. They asked, 'Were criminals bad by nature, or did circumstances force them into crime?' and 'Were some offenders victims, not criminals?'. Doctors observed that some criminals had mental problems that made it difficult for them to tell right from wrong. Other people realised that women and children might be bullied and forced to commit crimes.

Social scientists like Charles Booth (1840–1916) and Benjamin Rowntree (1871–1954) showed how poor people became trapped in miserable living conditions. They were not wicked but people with needs. Religious organisations like the Salvation Army (founded in 1865) worked hard to prove that even the worst criminals could be 'saved' from evil and live normal lives.

Novels and theories

Crime, and the nature of criminals, were also the subjects for some of the most popular Victorian novels. In *Dracula* (published 1897), Bram Stoker (1847–1912) invented a supernatural reason for monstrous behaviour. In *The Strange Case of Dr Jeckyll and Mr Hyde* (published 1886), Robert Louis Stevenson (1850–1894) suggested that all humans are born with the ability to choose between good and evil actions.

SERGEANT OF WOOD SHED.

MAT-MAKING SHED.

SERGEANT OF MAT-MAKERS.

THE SALVATION ARMY SOCIAL SCHEME: SKETCHES IN HANBURY STREET WHITECHAPEL.

Sketches of scenes from a Salvation Army industrial workshop for unemployed, homeless men in Whitechapel, London, in 1891. Workshops like this provided food and shelter in exchange for work until the men could find paid work for themselves. The Salvation Army hoped this would prevent people turning to crime to survive.

LASTING CHANGES

Victoria reigned for longer than any king or queen before her, and the Victorian age saw many changes in crime and punishments.

When Victoria came to the throne in 1837, crime was increasing rapidly. There were also workers' riots and political unrest. Many new kinds of crime were occuring, from trade union strikes to railway fare-dodging. Punishments for crime were severe. There was not yet a national prison system, and all prisoners were very harshly treated.

Crime in 1901

By the end of Victoria's reign, society had changed and there was less crime. Many people were still poor, but fewer were unemployed or starving. New, compulsory

A modern reconstruction of the 19th-century courtroom at Inveraray in Scotland. Lawyers (in wigs and gowns) make speeches accusing a prisoner (standing in the dock). Today visitors can explore Inveraray gaol and courtroom to find out what life was like there in Victorian times.

Criminal Statistics in 1889

Convicts in prisons	11,660
People in local prisons	20,883
Children convicted of crime in reformatories	1,270
Children in industrial schools	21,413
Criminal lunatics under restraint	910
Known thieves at large	14,747
Known receivers of stolen goods	1,121
Suspected persons	17,042
Total	**89,046**

From William Booth, *In Darkest England*, 1890.

schooling kept children busy all day. There were fewer riots; since 1867, working-class men could vote to make their political views known. In cities and towns, there were settled communities where working families took pride in law-abiding behaviour. Crime had not disappeared, of course. There were still shop-lifters, muggers, vandals, frauds and cunning professional criminals, just as there are today.

Policing and detection

Britain had new regional police forces. They were not perfect; there were worrying numbers of unsolved crimes, such as shocking murders by serial killer 'Jack the Ripper' in 1888. But policemen did deter offenders and catch many criminals. There were detectives with new skills, helped by new detection techniques.

Prison reform

Prison hulks had gone, transportation had ended and hangings were much less common. There were new national standards that improved conditions in prisons and new secure schools to reform young offenders. These standards still provide a basic framework for prison conditions, early in the 21st century.

Like politicians, doctors and other experts today, Victorian people still did not understand why some people became criminals. But Victorian lawyers, politicians, campaigners and charity workers were, slowly, making progress in understanding the many and complicated causes of crime.

Changing Crime Patterns

Crimes that decreased in Victoria's reign:
- Murder
- Riot
- Theft
- Assault (attack)
- Breach of the peace (public disturbance)
- Drunkenness
- Children's crime

Crimes that increased:
- Burglary
- Robbery with violence (mugging)
- Fraud and other commercial crimes

Victorian police stations had a blue lamp hanging outside them, so that victims of crime could find help quickly. Today, police patrol cars are fitted with flashing blue lights, and some police stations, like this Victorian one in Penge, London, keep their historic blue lights burning.

abolish get rid of something by introducing a new law.

assize court a court where judges and jurors meet to hear serious cases.

Chartist a member of a political movement called Chartism, which demanded reform of Parliament.

conviction the decision that someone is guilty of a crime.

debt the state of owing someone money.

debtor someone who owes money to another.

economist an expert in the production and use of goods and services.

embezzlement to steal money or goods that someone else has given you to look after.

fraud telling lies to get something valuable.

gallows an upright frame with a beam from which someone is hanged.

gaol a prison.

home secretary the government minister responsible for the law.

jury a group of people who must decide whether a person charged in a court has committed a crime.

magistrate a local judge.

mugger someone who attacks a person to steal from them.

night watchman someone appointed by a town to walk the streets at night and protect people from criminals.

petition a document asking people in power to do something specific.

poaching taking wild animals that were kept by someone else to be hunted.

prosecute to bring legal action against someone suspected of a crime.

protection racket threatening to harm someone if they do not pay money to prevent it.

reformer a person who tries to improve the way people are treated.

slum housing unfit for human habitation.

strike to stop working for an employer in order to get more money or better working conditions.

transported sent to a British colony overseas after being convicted of a crime.

truncheon a heavy wooden stick carried by a police officer.

witness someone who has seen a crime being committed.

workhouse an unpleasant refuge where the very poor had to live if they had no money.

1829 Metropolitan Police Force set up.

1834 Poor Law establishes workhouses for the very poor throughout the country, treating them as criminals.

1835 Checks on health and hygiene conditions in prisons are introduced.

1837 Victoria becomes queen.

1839 Chartist uprisings.

1842 Metropolitan Police uses trained detectives.

1844 A surveyor general of prisons is appointed; controls for building new prisons are introduced

1854 Reform schools set up.

1856 Police forces set up in all regions.

1865 New national rules for harsh treatment of prisoners.

1866 Industrial schools set up to train children at risk of becoming criminals.

1867 Last transportation to British colonies.

1868 Executions moved from public places into prisons.

1869 Imprisonment for debt abolished; National Criminal Record set up.

1876 Industrial day schools introduced.

1877 London detectives organised into Criminal Investigation Department

1898 Crank and treadmill abolished in prisons.

1900 Youth prisons set up.

1901 Fingerprints used to identify criminals; Queen Victoria dies.

PLACES TO VISIT

Greater Manchester Police Museum
http://www.gmp.police.uk/mainsite/pages/history.htm
Set in an old police station, there are Victorian cells with wooden pillows, the charge office, the magistrates court and historic police equipment and uniforms. Exhibits on forgery and forensic science.

Inveraray Jail
http://www.inverarayjail.co.uk
Visit the original courtroom with models and a soundtrack; see the airing yards where prisoners could be exercised; and walk around the new prison (1848), where prisoners were kept in separate cells.

Judge's Lodging, Presteigne
http://www.judgeslodging.org.uk
Radnorshire's restored shire hall includes the judge's apartments, servants' quarters, damp cells and a vast courtroom. Take an audiotour with voices from the past.

NCCL Galleries of Justice, Nottingham
http://www.galleriesofjustice.org.uk
Witness a trial in the original Victorian courtroom and visit the original prison cells, laundry, medieval caves and authentic prison exercise yard.

http://vcp.e2bn.org/index.php
This website is all about crime and punishment in the 19th-century in Bedfordshire and Cambridgeshire. It includes a prisoner database with actual prisoner records and case studies for a more in-depth view of the crimes and trials of some of the inmates. It also has sections on gaols – details about the buildings, daily life, gaol routines, inmates and staff.

http://history.powys.org.uk
The history of mid-Wales from photographs, documents, maps and museum exhibits. 'Victorian Powys' for schools includes topics such as workhouses and looks at crime and punishment in 18 small towns. 'Powys: a Day in the Life' compares life in 1891 with the present.

http://www.bbc.co.uk/history/british/victorians
The Victorians section of the BBC website. Sections include 'Crime and the Victorians', 'Victorian Mugshots Gallery', 'On the beat in Birmingham' and 'Beneath the Surface: A Country of Two Nations'.

http://www.learningcurve.gov.uk/victorianbritain/lawless/default.htm
From The National Archives. This website provides primary resources such as documents and historical pictures for you to decide whether Britain was a lawless nation.

http://www.workhouses.org.uk
A very comprehensive website about all the workhouses in Britain, the lives and recollections of their staff and inmates, workhouse rules and buildings and the Poor Law.

Note to parents and teachers: Every effort has been made by the Publishers to ensure that these websites are suitable for children, that they are of the highest educational value, and that they contain no inappropriate or offensive material. However, because of the nature of the Internet, it is impossible to guarantee that the contents of these sites will not be altered. We strongly advise that Internet access is supervised by a responsible adult.

INDEX

✸